LEVEL FIVE

COACHING COMMUNICATION SKILLS

UNLEASH THE POWER OF PROFESSIONAL COACHING CONVERSATIONS

Dan Luckett

John Hoskins

ISBN: 978-1-64184-778-0 (Paperback)
ISBN: 978-1-64184-779-7 (Ebook)

Contents

Dedication v

Foreword ix

Introduction—Expertise Is Not Enough...............................xi
    Food for Thought xii

Level 5 Coaching Communication Skills...............................1
    The Case for Specialized Coaching Communication Skills ...1
    How many skills are we talking about, and what are they? 2
    The Four Skill Areas 2
    Is that all there is?...3
    Can you use Coaching Communication Skills
        in everyday non-coaching situations?...........................4
    How we will approach the skills: 4

The Professional Coaching Skill of *Active Listening* 5
    Why Listen More Actively 5
    When to Listen Actively 5
    How to Listen Actively...6
    What makes listening difficult? 9
    Test Your Understanding 12

The Professional Coaching Skill of *Expressing Praise*..................17
    Why Express Praise...17
    When to Express Praise 18
    How to Express Praise 18
    What makes *Expressing Praise* difficult? 19
    Timing..20
    Test Your Understanding 23

The Professional Coaching Skill of *Expressing Concern*..................27

    Why Express Concern..27

    When to Express Concern 27

    How to Express Concern......................................28

    What makes expressing concern difficult? 30

    Test Your Understanding.....................................32

The Professional Coaching Skill of *Inviting Innovation*..................37

    Why Invite Innovation...37

    When to Invite Innovation 38

    How to Invite Innovation......................................39

    Test Your Understanding.....................................44

    What makes innovation difficult?...........................48

Deliberate Professionalism..49

Questions for Reflection...51

    Questions for Reflection about *The Case for Professional Communication Skills*...................................52

    Questions for Reflection about *Active Listening*......53

    Questions for Reflection about *Expressing Praise* ...54

    Questions for Reflection about *Expressing Concern*..................55

    Questions for Reflection about *Inviting Innovation* 56

Dedication

Donald A. Cook, Ph.D. (1927 – 1996)

The proverb, "*When the student is ready the teacher will appear,*" is variously ascribed to Buddhist and Confucian traditions. Regardless of its origins, it has meaning for me on several levels. At its most literal level, it describes my experience as a student at Columbia University in 1967. Dr. Cook was, for me, that one teacher who made all the difference. At that time, I was a veteran of two other schools and three different majors, none of which captured my imagination or inspired me to great effort. In Cook's course "Behavior Theory and Instructional Technology," I found direction for my academic pursuits. That course and subsequent studies at Columbia evolved into a friendship and a professional collegial relationship that lasted 29 years. Donald Cook was among the pioneers who took the findings from the laboratory study of learning into real-world, practical instructional design. He was one of the founders of Basic Systems, the company that became well-known as Xerox Learning Systems (XLS). Years later, I felt honored to follow in Donald's footsteps as I led the Product Development group at XLS for much of my 17-year tenure.

As a university professor, Donald was admired by his students for illuminating the connections between laboratory discoveries about behavior change and real-world learning mechanisms. His witty, entertaining classes told the scientific and technical stories along with the political and social context in which they occurred. On a couple of occasions, years later, Donald invited me as a guest speaker to his classes at Columbia and at SUNY Stony Brook. I relished those occasions, and I always felt that I got more than I gave in those classes.

Dear reader: If you are lucky enough to have had a special teacher appear for you when you were ready, please tell him or her while you still can. In my opinion, it doesn't get any better than that for an educator.

Dan Luckett

Dedication

Richard Ruff, Ph.D.

If you asked me the secret to success in business and life, my first advice would be to *pick the right partners*. I have had the good fortune of choosing the right partners both in business and in life. Richard (Dick) Ruff, Ph.D., is one of those right partners.

I first met Dick in the mid-nineties while visiting the Huthwaite farm in Leesburg, Virginia. Our Advantage Performance Group franchisees were being certified to sell SPIN and other capabilities Huthwaite offered. Dick was then, as he is now, erudite when discussing sales or sales leadership. Between Dick presenting and Neil Rackham doing his colorful layered overheads, our entire team couldn't wait to get back to our respective territories and begin to sell the Huthwaite IP.

Fast-forward two decades later; we had a chance meeting in line at Starbucks in Scottsdale in April of 2016. We decided to have coffee, and that conversation led to something much bigger and better than either of us could have realized. About a year later, we formed Level Five Selling, LLC. Dick jumped in with both feet and created an immense amount of quality content in record time. He spearheaded the entire animation, avatar, microlearning idea. Frankly, the Level Five Coaching System IP that Dick and I developed (with help from Janet Spirer, his life partner) remains a breakthrough approach in developing sales talent. It is unlike any other method we know.

We invested our seed capital and worked together to play to each other's strengths. We divided and conquered to build IP and a network of quality reseller partners. We hosted three very successful marketing deep-dives to immerse prospective clients in the system. That helped us land new clients and onboard new partners.

Dick and I never quarreled about investment in the business. We bootstrapped it and rolled tens of thousands of dollars back into the company to make it scale quickly. He never flinched. I am grateful for picking great partners in my past business ventures—people like Glenn Jackson, Dick Hodge, Ed Shineman, and Bob Conti. Dick is in that same major league of prolific entrepreneurs who do the right thing, innovate, live the values, and work tirelessly. And, we had fun and shared laughs along the way.

So, I dedicate this book to Dick. I am indebted to him for his partnership and many contributions to Level Five. We wouldn't be where we are today without his many contributions.

Thank you, partner.

John Hoskins

Foreword

I've spent my career analyzing high-performing sales leaders and salespeople, seeking to answer this question: **What separates the very best from the average to poor performers?**

As a chief sales officer, I found it perplexing to have several highly talented sales leaders executing the same strategy, with some receiving dramatically better results than others. How could that be? I discovered that sales leaders who consistently perform at the top of their game are collaborative coaches and outstanding communicators.

Co-Authors Dan Luckett and John Hoskins offer four powerful skills that will help any sales leaders communicate in a way that builds commitment to improving. When you listen to conversations between high-performing sales leaders and their direct reports, you'll notice something special—they employ a collaborative approach to leading. They ask more than they tell. Rather than saying, "I'm the expert, so I'll diagnose what's wrong and suggest what you should do to develop," they say, "You're the one responsible for development. I'm responsible for helping you become more aware of your performance and expanding your developmental choices." They reinforce strengths and are candid and straightforward when referring to deficiencies. The communication shifts from "I" and "You" to "We."

This book not only explains why high-performing leaders must be exceptional communicators but also describes how they do it. When you meet with these leaders, they are fully present, attentive, and listen to you at a 120 percent level. Communicating is both an art and science. Those who become proficient at these skills lead people to perform at their best.

John and Dan have provided an easy-to-follow, step-by-step formula to help you become a masterful communicator when coaching your salespeople to peak performance. Communication skills sound easy, yet you must practice them like any skill. Nearly every high-performing leader I've known has done just that. So, take these insights to heart and begin practicing them intentionally every day at work or home. You'll see a marked difference in how others respond to your coaching.

David Pearson
CEO, Level Five Selling

Introduction—Expertise Is Not Enough

This book is about raising your communication practices to a professional level. Let me tell you about a very brief experience I had a few years ago that led me to reflect on the concept of professionalism.

I board a plane late in the afternoon, very tired and keenly aware that the boredom and discomforts of travel will be mine well into the evening. We are still on the ground, but I am already tired. Too tired to focus on any work-related material, I seek escape in the airline magazine I find in the seat pocket. The entertainment value is meager, but it is the only escapist material I have. A fellow passenger standing in the aisle needs to get past me to his window seat. As I stand to accommodate him, I see that he is an airline captain; he neatly folds his uniform jacket, places it in the overhead bin, and settles in his seat. He retrieves a paperback novel from his flight bag and stows the bag under the seat in front of him. I am jealous. I know that this airline magazine will only amuse me for another 10 minutes at best. I mentally scold myself, *How could a seasoned road-warrior business traveler like me let himself get in such a bad situation avoidably unprepared?*

What's this? The captain puts his book aside unopened and starts rummaging through the seat pocket. What could he possibly think he will find? He pulls out the laminated, folded card that shows how to fasten seat belts and the location of emergency exits, life vests, and other safety instructions. Over the next 10 to 15 seconds, he very quickly, methodically, looks at, and runs his hand over each panel of the card. He purposefully looks around the cabin and then restores the card to the seat pocket. Then, he picks up his book. This seems crazy to me. He knows everything about this plane; he can fly it! He must find himself dead-heading in the passenger cabin several times every week. He is at least three times the road warrior that I am. Whenever the flight attendants perform their safety demonstrations, I pretend to pay attention out of courtesy, not genuine interest. All this safety material and the demonstrations are for first-time or occasional travelers—not for me, who has seen it all too often, who flies enough to earn free trips and upgrades.

Food for Thought

I put away the airline magazine.

Maybe I have been a bit too smug. Am I ready if there is an emergency evacuation of the plane? Even the captain was not above giving himself a quick refresher of the layout.

What are the odds that on this particular flight there will be an emergency evacuation? Vanishingly slight ... but ... not zero. Slight enough to be *not worth the trouble*? How much trouble are we talking about? Fifteen seconds? I have nothing better to do anyway. My internal argument with myself continues, *If there is going to be an emergency evacuation, there will be some warning, but maybe there will be smoke in the cabin, panicked passengers rising in their seats, lights failing, overhead bins popping open, and worse!* Okay, okay. Under those conditions, I would be glad I had reviewed the emergency exit row locations ahead of time.

How could a seasoned road-warrior business traveler like me let himself get in such a bad situation avoidably unprepared?

So why, of all the passengers on this plane, is the one passenger with the most aviation expertise very likely the only one reviewing this simple information—just in case?

In a word: ***professionalism.***

If you fly a lot, you may have noticed this. Before every flight, either the captain or co-pilot does a pre-check that involves walking around and under the aircraft with a flashlight in hand. She examines control surfaces, landing gear, hatches, tires, and more.

From the cockpit, she tests electronic and mechanical systems and runs through printed copies of very familiar checklists. Most of the steps are extremely simple: throw a switch, wiggle the wheel, test a warning light, read a fuel level, but she checks off each one because the stakes are high. The lives of the passengers are in her hands, and she's on the plane too. When a pilot rides as a passenger, some other easy steps also improve safety. As a professional, why not take those steps just as seriously? Professionalism often requires certain expertise with sophisticated information and processes—detailed knowledge or keenly refined skills that require long hours of practice. However, achieving the desired results may also depend on some simple but important steps based less on expertise and more on thoroughness and self-discipline. I wonder if the captain who sat next to me in the passenger cabin realized (or cared) that what I saw him do surprised me.

As a coach, your job consists of observing, processing what you observe based on your expertise and then communicating in a high-stakes collaboration. Your communication succeeds when it has the effect you intended it to have. But it can easily have no effect or even unintended negative effects. Consider the steps you will read about and practice here as items on a checklist. Once understood, they will seem simple, maybe even simple-minded. The checklist prevents you from forgetting or skipping any steps— if you have the will and self-discipline of a *professional sales coach*. When consistently applied, these steps will help prevent gaps between the effect you intend to have on those you coach and the effect you actually have. John and I have observed the enduring transformational power of these steps over many years and across every type of industry. We are excited to share them with you.

Dan Luckett

Level 5 Coaching Communication Skills

The Case for Specialized Coaching Communication Skills

As an educated adult, you certainly have the ability to communicate. You have been doing it with ever-increasing fluency since the day you were born. And, as a sales professional, you have become particularly skilled at managing a conversation and influencing other people. So what's left to learn about how to communicate?

Your effectiveness as a sales coach calls on your expertise in four challenging areas:

- **Product and industry** knowledge and experience
- All phases of the **sales process** from prospecting and strategy, through managing conversations with prospects and customers, to closing and implementing
- A **coaching model or process** for efficiently observing, monitoring, and influencing sales behavior and tracking results
- Coaching **communication skills** that enable you to give the benefits of your observations and technical and selling expertise and to be accepted as a coach.

Whatever level of product and industry knowledge you have, whatever your level of selling skill, however thorough your coaching model, 100 percent of what you can offer as a coach *must go through your communication with the person you coach.* Think of the coaching relationships and coaching challenges as very special situations calling for professionalized communication skills. If you fail to understand your sales professional's point of view, you stand little chance of winning him/her to your point of view. If you fail to explicitly call attention to your sales professional's strengths, progress, and successes, you squander opportunities to encourage more positive behavior. You also weaken the sales professional's trust that you are truly committed to their success. If you shrink from clearly and directly expressing disagreement or calling out counter-productive behavior, you deny your sales professionals the information they need to make progress. On the other hand, if you can establish and maintain collaborative coaching relationships with your salespeople, you can help them to flourish.

How many skills are we talking about, and what are they?

First, the good news: We will focus on only four skills, and each has just a few simple steps. Now, for the tricky part: Because you have been communicating your entire life, you will face constant temptation to revert to old habits; it will be up to you to set standards and monitor the professionalism of your communication.

The Four Skill Areas

The first skill is called ***Active Listening***. Communication involves both sending and receiving. Both are equally essential, and both are susceptible to a gap between intent and effect. *Active Listening* implies much more than merely hearing. It includes asking questions to complete and verify your understanding, and it also includes some essential mental work.

The second skill is called ***Expressing Praise***. We all know what praise is. Most of us would like to *get* more of it, and most of us would benefit—our work would benefit—from *giving* more of it. Yet, sometimes, people react to praise in surprising ways. And, sometimes, people seem reluctant to give praise, even though common sense suggests that giving praise should be a pleasant experience. You will learn a formula for providing sincere praise, with little or no gap between your intent and your likely effect.

We call the third skill ***Expressing Concern***. The common word for this is criticism. Differences in opinions, judgments, priorities, and expectations are all inevitable and essential. If we all saw everything the same way, we would have little to discuss, little to learn from one another, and little to contribute. Now, for obvious reasons, we don't always express our concerns to everyone we speak to. And pointing out errors, poor practices, or judgments can wreak collateral damage to self-esteem and trigger fear, defensiveness, or other counter-productive responses. But you owe candor to those whom you coach when you encounter behaviors and judgments that don't serve them well. So you will learn how to *Express Concern* in a way that adds value and minimizes the risk of a gap between your intent and your effect.

Inviting Innovation is the name we have given to the fourth skill. Today's organizations depend on the ability to innovate. Innovation can mean inventing a blockbuster product or devising a slightly more efficient way to complete a familiar step. For a sales professional, it might mean adding a new prospecting tool or revising a sales call agenda. Innovation does not have to be of historic or revolutionary magnitude to be important. In the past, innovation may have been expected of sales superstars. Today, and on into the future, innovation has become table stakes—the price of admission—the essence of the job. As a coach, it is not enough for you to pass along innovative tips of the trade. Rather, you must collaborate to model the process of innovation itself. By using your communication skills, you can encourage your salesperson's engagement with, and ownership of, their challenges.

Of course, an individual working alone certainly may come up with a valuable innovation. But sales coaching, by its nature, requires collaboration, so we will focus on managing conversations to nurture and facilitate <u>collaboration to produce innovation</u>.

Is that all there is?

These four skills do not comprise a complete list of communications tools for every situation. You may have other communications challenges that have nothing to do with coaching and that call for tools specialized for those situations. However, for the challenge of collaborating to enhance sales performance, these four skills will multiply your effectiveness while minimizing unintended effects.

It will not be enough for you to memorize the skills and the three or four steps for each one. Some of these steps may come naturally to you, but others may not. You will also need to do the work to enable new habits that may conflict with old ones. By completing the exercises at the end of each chapter, you can start to take ownership of these skills.

Can you use Coaching Communication Skills in everyday non-coaching situations?

Absolutely! Remember when you had your first selling skills training and then discovered that your newfound selling skills could help with non-selling conversations as well? Like your selling skills, these coaching skills are powerful tools for effective communication in a wide range of situations both personal and professional. Learn them to help you coach, and then use them whenever they seem to fit your intent.

How we will approach the skills:

For each skill, we will consider *why* it is important and necessary. Then, we will examine the cues to use the skill—the *when*. Next, comes the *how* section that describes the three or four *steps* that make up the skill and the rationale for each step. Then, we will consider the *difficulties* that make that skill challenging to implement. These skills are deceptively simple, but that does not mean that they are easy to own. Finally, we will engage in some skills *practice*. The only way to learn to do something is to do it.

The Professional Coaching Skill of *Active Listening*

Why Listen More Actively

As sales leaders, we have plenty of excuses for not actively listening: time pressures, distractions, interruptions, and a to-do list a mile long. However, deliberately listening 120 percent can pay significant dividends for your coaching effectiveness. As the Greek philosopher Diogenes suggested, "We have two ears and one tongue so that we would listen more and talk less." Just as a successful sales professional talks less and listens more when calling on customers, the same is true for sales leaders who engage in coaching conversations.

We coach by communicating, and that requires both sending and receiving. How skillfully you listen (receive) has a tremendous impact on the accuracy and completeness of the communication. And *if you base your actions or your decisions* on inaccurate or incomplete communication, you may experience unintended consequences.

When to Listen Actively

- When you will take action or make a decision
- When you feel triggered to reject, ignore, or disagree with what someone has done or said

You can never go wrong by listening actively, but the two situations listed above give important cues that should grab your attention. Let's consider these two situations that demand your most professional listening.

First, when you take action based on your understanding of what you hear, it raises the stakes. Your simple misunderstanding can lead to misguided action and choices, which in turn lead to poor outcomes.

Second, when what you hear triggers your impulse to *reject, ignore, or disagree* with what you hear, you may say or do something that interferes with your intention to understand; you may even interfere with your relationship with the person you are coaching. Can you consistently demonstrate extremely focused, deliberate listening every minute of every day? Probably not. But these two cues will tell you when highly professional listening will pay off the most.

How to Listen Actively

Three behaviors can close the gap between your intent to accurately capture another person's message to you and the misunderstandings that can interfere. These same behaviors will convey your sincere intent to capture the other person's meaning.

Step 1: Presume Value

The first step in *Active Listening* does not tell you what to *say*; rather, it tells you what to *think*. While you cannot hear or see yourself doing this step, you can know if you are doing it.

For example, suppose you are discussing a performance challenge with a sales professional you coach. That person contributes an idea or piece of information to the conversation. And let's say that the contribution strikes you as illogical or irrelevant to the task at hand, or at least inadequate. In other words, *you feel triggered to reject, ignore, or disagree.* Now, if you stop to think about it, you know that the person you are talking with is intelligent, sane, and motivated to address the challenge. However flawed, is it really likely that the contribution has absolutely no value whatsoever? At the very least, that contribution tells you something useful about the contributor's level of knowledge about the challenge or certain restrictions or resources. But even if you see no particular value in the contribution, you can start to look for the value if you *presume value*. On the other hand, if you presume that because you don't see any value, there must not be any value, are you likely to look for it? Your assumptions—what goes on in your head as you hear some-one—will likely control how actively you listen. Presuming value is not something you say. It is something you check with yourself about to make sure you are doing it. Presuming value will influence what you say in the next step.

Step 2: Explore the *What* and *Why*

In the second step, you ask questions. Now that you are presuming value, let's try to find it. Think of this step as starting an investigation.

You don't see the value, but like a detective with suspicions, you are pretty sure—you presume—you can find it. Exploring the "what" of a contribution fills in gaps, corrects misunderstandings, and adds details. You might ask, "How would you make that happen?" or, "Could you explain more about how that would work?" Exploring the "why" of a contribution helps clarify the contributor's reasoning. You might ask, "How would that get us closer to our goal of accomplishing X?" or, "Have you ever tried something like that?"

Of course, if you did see value in the suggestion from the start, you may find listening a bit easier. Exploring *what* and *why* will still serve you well as you plan or act based on what you hear. How deep should your investigation go? Investigate at least deeply enough to enable you to go to the next step, which is to *verify* your understanding.

Step 3: Verify the *What* and *Why*

When you have discovered the *What* and *Why* of the idea or action, including the value that the contributor of the idea intended to communicate, go to the final step of *Active Listening* and *Verify* your understanding. Now, you might understand the value of an idea and still have concerns about it. In a later chapter of this book, you will learn the skill of *Expressing Concern*. But if you feel that the idea has promise, you can collaborate to take advantage of that promise. Whether you saw the value in the contribution from the start, or you needed to investigate to overcome your impulse *to reject, ignore, or disagree* with the contribution, the *Verify* step will enable you to check your understanding and to demonstrate that you understand. If you missed some part or got it wrong, then the contributor can correct you, and you can try verifying again. Even though much of conversation consists of correcting misunderstandings, misconceptions remain frequent and sometimes very costly.

That's it!

- Presume value
- Explore
- Verify (what and why)

What makes listening difficult?

We take in information, seemingly through our senses, and we respond to that information with thoughts and actions. But the information that we take in does not all come to us through our senses. Our brains build our experience of incoming information from two sources:

- Incoming sensory data
- Old, stored experiences about what *usually* accompanies specific incoming sensory data

Our brains <u>seamlessly</u> combine data from these two sources into something that feels (very convincingly) like a single version of our ongoing experience. For example: If one of your sales professionals says to you "these call reports are not a good use of my time..." you may find it difficult to actively listen to what follows. You may feel that you have already heard everything that can be said on this subject. If your brain has already supplied the rest of this idea you may feel that your stored version is identical to whatever the salesperson says next. This phenomenon of old, stored experience combining seamlessly with incoming sensory data provides the mechanism for many optical illusions.

The good news is that this built version of experience often gives us a more coherent story that serves us better than a version with all the gaps, noise, and distractions of a raw sensory feed.

The bad news is that the old experiences that we stir in often introduce errors. The old experiences do not perfectly match the current circumstances, and by the way, we built those old experiences as well. So, errors in old perceptions beget more errors.

Passive Listening means accepting our initial built version of a message, errors and all.

Active Listening means doing the professional work (presumptions and questions) to catch those errors and build a much more accurate and complete version of the communication. Everyone does this to some extent. Professionals deliberately do this, especially when the temptation to dismiss is high or when the stakes are high.

Other barriers also interfere with listening. One physical challenge is the average rate of speech. Culturally, Western world speech is about 125 words per minute. However, the human brain can process about 800 words per minute. So, words enter our brains at a much slower speed, and we continue to think at high speed. That's when we easily get distracted. That's all the more reason for the verification steps. When our attention lapses, an even greater share of our listening experience is built from old information that may be incorrect. *Verifying* can catch those errors and give us a second chance to get it right.

TEST YOUR UNDERSTANDING

Instructions:

Underline questions by the coach to *explore*, and circle questions by the coach to *verify*.

Sales professional:	I didn't press her about the service contract.
Coach:	Didn't we agree that you would try to convert this account to the new service contract with remote monitoring? What did you say about the service contract idea?
Sales professional:	I explained that with our new service contract, she could prevent most unplanned shutdowns. She asked how much it would save on repairs and replacements. So, I explained that the benefit was not so much about saving money on repairs and replacements but rather preventing the disruption of unplanned shutdowns. The problem is she's more concerned about out-of-pocket costs than anything else.
Coach:	But we could show her, with numbers, how much more those unplanned shutdowns cost. You need to get her to see the bigger picture. Would she agree to us doing an audit?
Sales professional:	No.

Coach:	So the costs of the contract, along with the parts and replacements that she would still pay for, are more important to her than the disruptions to production.
Sales professional:	Apparently so. I think she is evaluated mostly on the direct monthly cost of maintenance and repairs. She also seemed concerned that early detection of likely pump failures would lead to more frequent replacements versus waiting until something breaks. We might replace a pump that was still working.
Coach:	So, if I understand you correctly, this customer was more interested in keeping direct maintenance and repair costs low than in preventing disruptions to production, even if those disruptions were far more costly in terms of lost production and wasted raw materials?
Sales professional:	Yes. I could tell that she didn't want to talk about it.
Coach:	And you think her priorities are driven by how she is evaluated. So you felt that engaging her further about a service contract would only annoy her.
Sales professional:	Right.

Answer Key

Instructions:

Underline questions by the coach to _explore_, and circle questions by the coach to (verify.)

Sales professional:	I didn't press her about the service contract.
Coach:	Didn't we agree that you would try to convert this account to the new service contract with remote monitoring?
	What did you say about the service contract idea?
Sales professional:	I explained that with our new service contract, she could prevent most unplanned shutdowns. She asked how much it would save on repairs and replacements. So I explained that the benefit was not so much about saving money on repairs and replacements, but rather preventing the disruption of unplanned shutdowns. The problem is she's more concerned about out-of-pocket costs than anything else.
Coach:	But we could show her, with numbers, how much more those unplanned shutdowns cost. You need to get her to see the bigger picture. Would she agree to us doing an audit?
Sales professional:	No.

Coach:	So the costs of the contract, along with the parts and replacements that she would still pay for, are more important to her than the disruptions to production.
Sales professional:	Apparently so. I think she is evaluated mostly on the direct monthly cost of maintenance and repairs. She also seemed concerned that early detection of likely pump failures would lead to more frequent replacements versus just waiting until something breaks. We might replace a pump that was still working.
Coach:	So, if I understand you correctly, this customer was more interested in keeping direct maintenance and repair costs low than in preventing disruptions to production – even if those disruptions were far more costly in terms of lost production and wasted raw materials?
Sales professional:	Yes. I could tell that she didn't want to talk about it.
Coach:	And you think her priorities are driven by how she is evaluated. So you felt that engaging her further about a service contract would only annoy her.
Sales professional:	Right.

The Professional Coaching Skill of *Expressing Praise*

Will you coach to correct weaknesses in performance or to build on strengths? Why not do both? Feedback about current or past performance provides valuable information to guide improvement efforts. The people you coach cannot treat every aspect of how they work as equally in need of improvement. They need to focus their attention to make changes that will provide the most benefit. At the same time they need to hold on to, and build on, the things they do best. As a coach, you observe behavior to compare your observations with what your expertise tells you about best practices. Later, we will consider how you *express concerns*. For now, let's consider how (and even *if*) you express praise.

Sales leaders tend to underuse the critical skill of providing recognition for a job well-done. This is unfortunate because salespeople with high self-esteem are more motivated, confident, likely to perform well, and more likely to stay. When you praise someone, you are reinforcing the importance of meeting and exceeding expectations. When you fail to express deserved praise, you squander a very valuable opportunity.

Why Express Praise

It rewards desired behavior, making it more likely to be repeated.

It enhances confidence, self-esteem, and motivation of the person you coach.

- It enhances the collaborative relationship.
- It helps you retain your most high-potential and productive team members.
- It provides valuable information.

But these benefits do not happen automatically in response to praise. The effectiveness of praise depends on how the recipients of the praise understand and interpret the praise.

- Will they believe that your praise is sincere?
- Will they connect the praise with specific efforts?
- Does the praise align with their own assessment of their work?

It's easy to spot someone underperforming. But the greater opportunity lies with catching someone doing something right. Then, you can seize the moment to reinforce positive behaviors and results. Accurate and sincere praise inspires similar future behavior. On the other hand, inaccurate or non-specific praise will likely feel half-hearted, possibly manipulative, and certainly unprofessional.

When to Express Praise

Give praise when you appreciate the quality, reliability, or improvement in someone's work.

How to Express Praise

Here is an easy-to-follow formula for ensuring your praise is credible and effective. While you may not always include all four steps, each of these steps further enhances the clarity and power of your praise and reduces the odds of unintended effects. For maximum impact, include all four steps.

Step 1: Refer to Praise-Worthy Performance

Desirable outcomes can result from various combinations of causes: intentional efforts, luck, efforts of others, and coincidence. But if the actions of the recipient of your praise played a pivotal role, your praise should focus on those specific, observable actions. And don't forget that sometimes great work results in disappointing results. Bad luck, coincidence, and unrelated events can all intervene. But good performance, even when it leads to poor results, deserves praise.

Step 2: Cite Examples

If the praise-worthy performance occurred over a long period of time, citing specific examples can enhance perceived sincerity and credibility. You may not know of, or recall, all of the action contributing to the praise-worthy performance, but the more examples the better. If you don't know enough of the details, do your homework. Check old reports or your calendar to jog your memory. Ask others who saw, or benefited from, the performance. Feel free to cite second-hand praise from others.

Step 3: Connect to Personal Qualities

Connecting praise-worthy performance to personal qualities enhances confidence to support future strong performance.

Examples of personal qualities might include:

- Expertise or skill in a particular area
- Empathy
- Patience
- Persistence

The personal qualities that you cite should be qualities under the person's control. Do not cite qualities not under a person's control, such as height, age, or ethnicity.

Step 4: Connect to Goals

Connecting praise-worthy performance to your goals, the recipient's goals, or the organization's goals acknowledges the value of the praise-worthy performance. Be clear about what this performance will contribute.

What makes *Expressing Praise* difficult?

Common sense suggests that *Expressing Praise* ought to be easy. What's not to like about giving someone good news about their work or idea? It turns out that praise can lead to unintended effects. A 2010 study published in the "Journal of Experimental Social Psychology" found that nearly 70 percent of study subjects "associate embarrassment or discomfort with the process of being recognized." The reasons given varied but were often related to doubts about the sincerity of the praise or regrets about not having done even better.

Similarly, reluctance to give praise may have a variety of sources. Many feel awkward giving praise. Some may feel that the salary, commissions, and perks are ample praise. Some who feel uncomfortable receiving praise think others feel the same way. Some may feel that they have worked hard and received little or no praise, and others should do the same. And some may worry that the recipient of praise will become complacent and less eager to strive harder. Much of what makes it difficult lies within you. But the more you prepare to deliver praise supported by facts and sincere appreciation, the easier praising becomes.

When praise was couched in "concrete language rather than abstract language," experimenters in the above-cited study found a significant reduction in negative perceptions of praise. In other words, be *specific*. Non-specific praise can seem patronizing to the recipient. Using short-cut terms like "terrific" or "fantastic" may seem like extreme language masking a thoughtless response. The steps for giving effective praise mostly have to do with ways to be specific. So crafting a statement of praise will take some time and work. But your work will be rewarded when it conveys your sincerity.

Timing

Sometimes, you will give praise on the spot—as soon as you discover the praise-worthy performance. But fortunately, you can become an expert giver of praise without having to craft perfect praise statements on the fly. *Expressing Praise* readily lends itself to preparation. You can express praise in the back-and-forth flow of conversation, but you can also express praise with a carefully crafted written statement. Written praise carries a special weight;

however, spoken praise, if properly crafted, will also provide valuable guidance and encouragement. Take your time. Even if you will deliver your praise verbally, you can plan it out ahead of time. Do your research; rehearse it. You might even make yourself a discreet cheat sheet.

TEST YOUR UNDERSTANDING

Instructions:

- **Circle references to praise-worthy performance**
- **Underline specific examples**
- **Put an * at the beginning of statements that connect praise-worthy performance to goals**
- **Put a "P" at the beginning of statements that connect to personal qualities**

To: Bob Cooper
From: Phyllis Jones
Subject: Lunch & Learn session at United Liquefied Enzyme

Phil, I want to give you some feedback on the Lunch & Learn session on Preemptive Maintenance Economics that I saw you deliver at ULE last Wednesday.

It seemed to me that it went extremely well. Your kickoff with a review of known issues, based on your advance conversations with key influencers, seemed to engage the group right from the start. You are very good at discovering each individual's priorities. Also, your explanations of bottom-line benefits were clear and concise. By drawing on your knowledge of production disruptions experienced at ULE in recent months, you were able to make the presentation relevant for all participants.

The way you verified your understanding of each question raised, before launching into your response, greatly impressed me. And your patience with Howard's somewhat tedious nitpicking struck the right balance between respecting his concerns, while making efficient use of the available time.

Your thorough preparation and professional delivery positioned us as a reliable partner. I think we are significantly closer to selling ULE on the Preemptive Maintenance program, and I look forward to hearing about your next steps.

Answer Key

Instructions:

- **Circle references to praise-worthy performance**
- **Underline specific examples**
- **Put an * at the beginning of statements that connect praise-worthy performance to goals**
- **Put a "P" at the beginning of statements that connect to personal qualities**

To: Bob Cooper
From: Phyllis Jones
Subject: Lunch & Learn session at United Liquefied Enzyme

Phil, I want to give you some feedback on the Lunch & Learn session on Preemptive Maintenance Economics that I saw you deliver at ULE last Wednesday.

It seemed to me that it went extremely well. Your kickoff with a review of known issues, based on your advance conversations with key influencers, seemed to engage the group right from the start. P You are very good at discovering each individual's priorities. Also, your explanations of bottom-line benefits were clear and concise. By drawing on your knowledge of production disruptions experienced at ULE in recent months, you were able to make the presentation relevant for all participants.

The way you verified your understanding of each question raised, before launching into your response, greatly impressed me. And you P patience with Howard's somewhat tedious nitpicking struck the right balance between respecting his concerns, while making efficient use of the available time.

Your thorough preparation and professional delivery positioned us as a reliable partner. *I think we are significantly closer to selling ULE on the Preemptive Maintenance program, and I look forward to hearing about your next steps.

Your Turn

Does *Expressing Praise* seem pretty simple now? There is no time like the present to give it a try. Draft a praise memo to someone who reports to you, someone you coach, or a family member. Choose someone who recently did something well that you appreciate. Include all four of the *Expressing Praise* steps for maximum effect. You may want to send this memo when you finish writing it, or you may use it as a guide when you deliver your praise verbally.

If the task turns out to be more challenging than you anticipated, ask yourself why.

The Professional Coaching Skill of *Expressing Concern*

Why Express Concern

In the book *Feedback (and Other Dirty Words)*, authors Chandler and Grealish reference a study by OfficeVibe that presents a paradox. Sixty-two percent of employees want more feedback, and 83 percent appreciate feedback, whether positive or negative. Numerous other studies indicate that organizations in which people seek, give, and receive feedback outperform financially, including margins, ROI, ROA, and ROE. In her book, *Radical Candor,* author and Silicon Valley executive Kim Scott documents her journey learning how to give and receive candid performance feedback through dozens of personal experiences.

Developing a coaching culture involves a healthy combination of expressing praise and expressing concerns. The people whom you coach need your feedback. When they perform well, when they express ideas and plans about their work that you agree with, you can praise their work and their thinking as appropriate. And when their performance needs changes or when you disagree with their thinking, they need to know your concerns as well. To quote Kim Scott, "You've been told since you learned to talk, 'If you don't have anything nice to say, don't say anything at all.' Now all of sudden it's your job to say it." Skillful candor need not be obnoxious or cruel.

When to Express Concern

If you have verified your understanding of an idea, request, or performance and it seems flawed or concerning to you, then you should express your concern. But if you have not yet verified your understanding, do that before you express your concern.

Expressing a concern based on misunderstanding wastes everyone's time and energy.

We saw earlier how important *Active Listening* is when:

- You will take action or make a decision.
- You feel triggered to reject, ignore, or disagree with what someone has done or said.

When you decide to *express concern*, it usually means that at least one of these conditions applies—probably both. You did not like some aspect of the behavior or statement that you will *express concern* about, and you have decided to take the action of saying so. *Active Listening* is the prerequisite for *Expressing Concern*.

How to Express Concern

Step 1: Verify Shared and/or Conflicting Goals

Goals describe what you want to accomplish. When you and the person who triggered your concern share the same goal, you will likely only disagree about methods. Acknowledging that you both are after the same thing sets a positive, collaborative tone. And if you have different goals, making those differences explicit brings clarity to the conversation. You can have different, or even conflicting, goals but still regard the other person's goals as legitimate and worthy of consideration. You can verify goals by simply stating, "I assume we both want to _____." Or, "What's important to me is to _____. What's most important for you?"

Step 2: Itemize Both Elements of Value and Your Concern(s)

Since you have decided to act and express your concerns, you will have engaged in *Active Listening*, which includes *Presuming Value, Exploring,* and *Verifying*. By presuming value, exploring, and verifying, you will be equipped to neutralize the other person's feelings that you don't understand. You will also be equipped to focus on the precise areas of concern and avoid seeming to criticize more broadly than you intend. Your concern(s) are justified by your shared, or at least mutually acknowledged, goals. Your *expressions of concern* can be very direct—even blunt—when you have done the work of *Active Listening* first. Combining your *expressions of concerns* with your perceptions of value is not about sugar-coating at all. Instead, it is all about precision and bringing to life your respect for the person you are coaching and that person's priorities. And it is about very specifically limiting your expression of concern and distinguishing your concerns from the value you perceive. In this way, you set the stage for the heart of the coaching collaboration, which is, "What shall we do to improve?"

Step 3: Invite/Offer Ways to Eliminate Concerns while Retaining Value

Sometimes, you may decide to simply tell the person you're coaching what your experience tells you is the best way forward. Other times, you may choose to invite innovation through creative collaboration. We will explore that option in the next chapter. Having chosen one of these paths, you may change your mind and switch to the other—just be sure to tell the individuals you are coaching what you are doing. If you feel committed to a certain next step, you should say so. But keep in mind that most people will more fully commit to a plan that they have a hand in creating. Do not try to lead others to come up with your idea. If you play the game of "guess what I am thinking," you risk appearing manipulative.

What makes expressing concern difficult?

It's damned if you do and damned if you don't. You have seen it happen. You express concern with the best of intentions, only to see the recipient of your feedback respond emotionally. The recipient may argue, become defensive, and seem visibly crushed. What you intended as helpful suggestions may be experienced as sweeping evidence of your low opinion of the person. The gap between your intent and your effect is enormous. If you <u>don't</u> express your concerns, you deny the recipient of your coaching crucial information. And if you <u>do</u> express your concerns, you may trigger fear, sap motivation, or elicit other counter-productive reactions. Yet, by preceding your concern with *Active Listening* and by stating the value that you find in the concerning idea or performance, you can reduce or even eliminate the negative impact of expressing your concern. And by supporting the performer's ideas for overcoming your concerns, you can stay on a collaborative path.

The steps above for *Expressing Concern* not only facilitate accurate communication but also convey respect and the sincerity of your coaching intentions.

Test Your Understanding

Instructions:

- **Underline questions or statements by the coach to verify shared or conflicting goals.**
- **Mark with a "*V*" any statement to itemize *Value***
- **Mark with a "*C*" any statement to itemize *Concern(s)***
- **Mark with "*I/O*" any statement to *invite or offer* ways to eliminate concerns while retaining value**

Coach:	So, if I understand you correctly, this customer was more interested in keeping direct maintenance and repair costs low than in preventing disruptions to production, even if those disruptions were far more costly in terms of lost production and wasted raw materials?

Sales professional:	Yes. I could tell that she didn't want to talk about it.

Coach:	And you think her priorities are driven by how she is evaluated. So you felt that engaging her further about a service contract would only annoy her.

Sales professional:	Right.

Coach:	I think we agree that we want to sell our new Preemptive Maintenance program to all our customers for whom it makes sense.

Sales professional:	Yes.

Coach:	And do we agree that the program would greatly benefit this customer, both operationally and economically?
Sales professional:	Yes.
Coach:	And I certainly agree with you that we don't want to annoy this maintenance manager, or try to get her to act against her own best interests.
Sales professional:	That's the bind.
Coach:	I am concerned that we are not making progress here with selling the program. So we need a way to get the company to see that the criteria for evaluating this maintenance manager have become misaligned with the company's goals.
Sales professional:	That would be great.
Coach:	Do you have any ideas about how we could do that without damaging your relationship with the maintenance manager?

Answer Key

Instructions:

- **Underline questions or statements by the coach to verify shared or conflicting goals.**
- **Mark with a "*V*" any statement to itemize *Value***
- **Mark with a "*C*" any statement to itemize *Concern(s)***
- **Mark with "*I/O*" any statement to *invite or offer* ways to eliminate concerns while retaining value**

Coach:	So, if I understand you correctly, this customer was more interested in keeping direct maintenance and repair costs low than in preventing disruptions to production – even if those disruptions were far more costly in terms of lost production and wasted raw materials?

Sales professional:	Yes. I could tell that she didn't want to talk about it.

Coach:	And you think her priorities are driven by how she is evaluated. So you felt that engaging her further about a service contract would only annoy her.

Sales professional:	Right.

Coach:	I think we agree that we want to sell our new Preemptive Maintenance program to all our customers for whom it makes sense.

Sales professional:	Yes.

Coach:	And do we agree that the program would greatly benefit this customer, both operationally and economically?
Sales professional:	Yes.
Coach:	And I certainly agree with you that we don't want to annoy this maintenance manager, or try to get her to act against her own best interests.
Sales professional:	That's the bind.
Coach:	I am concerned that we are not making progress here with selling the program. So we need a way to get the company to see that the criteria for evaluating this maintenance manager have become misaligned with the company's goals.
Sales professional:	That would be great.
Coach: 1/0	Do you have any ideas about how we could do that without damaging your relationship with the maintenance manager?

The Professional Coaching Skill of *Inviting Innovation*

Why Invite Innovation

Sometimes, a goal seems just out of reach. Neither you nor the person you coach seem able to find a way to progress toward a particular goal. Maybe all of the options you have considered have unacceptable drawbacks, or maybe you tried several approaches with disappointing results. You need more options.

- How can you shorten the typical (or a particular) sales cycle?
- What's a clearer way to demonstrate a complex technical feature of your product?
- How can your sales professional stop inserting, "You know?" after every spoken sentence?
- How can your sales professional become less dependent on help from a financial expert in your company's marketing department?

With some deliberate effort, you can set the stage for a creative collaboration that may lead to a possible breakthrough innovation. Just as important, you want those you coach to become better at coming up with their own strategies for improvement. By engaging in creative collaboration with someone you coach, you set an example for seeking innovative solutions—for not settling for choosing among mediocre options. Coaching is not something you do *to* someone. It is also not something you can do *for* someone. Coaching skillfully means *helping* someone analyze their challenges and figure out strategies. In the words of Herminia Ibarra and Anne Scoular writing in "The Harvard Business Review" (November–December 2019):

> Twenty-first-century managers simply don't (and can't!) have all the right answers. To cope with

this new reality, companies are moving away from traditional command-and-control practices and toward something very different: a model in which managers give support and guidance rather than instructions.

When to Invite Innovation

- When a performer feels stuck and needs a breakthrough to overcome a performance challenge
- When you want additional or better options

How to Invite Innovation

Step 1: Verify Goals

By definition, you cannot know ahead of time what the innovation will look like, but you can know what you hope it will accomplish. Focus the conversation by verifying that all participants agree on the goal or goals sought. You might pursue two or more goals that initially seem mutually exclusive. In such cases, the goal becomes, "How can we achieve both?" or, "How can we achieve _____, while still _____?"

Example:

Sales professional:	
Coach:	… so you agree that at that point in the call, you launched into describing how we could solve a problem that the customer had <u>not</u> said that he had. Solutions without problems.
Sales professional:	Yeah, when I get nervous, I tend to do that. I know we've had this conversation before. I can't seem to stop doing it.
Coach:	What have you tried to control that behavior?
Sales professional:	Before a call, I make some notes in my Pre-Call Plan about the points I want to cover and the questions I want to ask. I started making the first item in my notes: **"Shut up and listen!"**
Coach:	Did that work at all?

Sales professional:	The first call I made with that topping my notes seemed to help. Every time my eye caught my "shut up..." note to self I kept probing deeper. But then I started to worry that the customer might get a peek at my notes, so I stopped doing it.
Coach:	So we need a way for you to remind yourself, without putting something potentially embarrassing at the top of your notes?
Sales professional:	Yes. I thought about writing my "shut up" note in Greek, but then what if my customer happened to be fluent in Greek.
Coach:	So let's set a goal of devising a note to self that will be loud and clear to you but meaningless and inconspicuous to anyone else—no matter what languages they know.
Sales professional:	Okay.

Step 2: Suspend Restrictions and Judgments

In his book *Hair Brain, Tortoise Mind*, research psychologist Guy Claxton describes recent research evidence for the effectiveness of various creative thinking strategies. Moreover, the research supports the theory that humans are capable of two radically different states of mind. Analyzing, calculating, evaluating, and judging all call for one type of mental activity. That is very different from the mental state that allows you to indulge your curiosity, to consider surprising connections, or to detect subtle patterns. That state of mind stops working if it is rushed or subjected to tight controls. Most of us spend much of our time in the former state—and quite properly so. In that state of mind, we can solve problems quickly, use mathematical tools and apply critical thinking. But the latter state is the one most likely to yield creative invention or insight. For most people, deciding to temporarily suspend or ignore the usual restrictions and disciplines requires a deliberate mental act. And a group or pair of collaborators is more likely to be able to set aside normal patterns if they explicitly agree to do so. You might say, "Let's pretend for a moment that we have no restrictions. What would we do?" or, "Let's brainstorm for a few minutes; no idea is too crazy." Also, this is not the time to express concerns. If an idea is put forward that triggers you to *Reject, Ignore or Disagree*, hold off *Expressing Concern* while restrictions are suspended. To stimulate your creative juices, you might suspend all restrictions or only the one or two restrictions that seem to block the flow of ideas. By the same token, limit your questions to verifying your understanding if necessary. The purpose of the no-restrictions discussion is to favor the quantity of ideas over quality. The spontaneous, curious, playful part of the brain does not do well under scrutiny. Hold off on in-depth exploring. While restrictions are suspended, all things are possible. You can weed out ideas that hold no promise later.

Step 3: Recognize and Connect Contributions, Ideas and Patterns

A new idea is like a newborn baby; if attacked, it will very likely not survive long enough to realize its potential. If a new idea (yours or someone else's) makes you think of all the reasons why the idea is useless or impossible, resist the impulse to throw it away. Instead, look for connections and patterns. Does an idea remind you of or give you another idea? You might consider (or ask) where the idea came from, where it might lead, or if it might suggest a pattern. One way to recognize an idea is simply to write it down. Another way is to state how another person's idea triggered an idea in your mind. Share not only your idea but also what triggered it. When you find and recognize connections between ideas that come from the other person and ideas you contribute, you get another benefit as well. You share credit for the new idea. When individuals you coach take ownership of innovation, their commitment to making it work increases. So it pays to be generous with credit for ideas.

Examples:

- "What you said about _____ led me to think about _____."
- "I like your idea of _____. What if we went even further and _____?"
- "Can I hitchhike on your idea about _____?"
- "If we did _____, would that be in line with your original idea of _____?"

Step 4: Express Patience

Sometimes you need to settle on a plan immediately, and sometimes you have the luxury of time to discover and consider more options. The creative part of your brain often does its best work when you sleep or when you focus on thoughts or activities that are irrelevant to your innovation challenge. To take advantage of that phenomenon, keep the process of seeking an innovation going for as long as you can afford to, but not longer. Remind yourself of the goal at least daily and then go about your business. Try to restate the goal. If the goal describes what you really want, ask yourself why you want it. What do you really, really, really want? Think of it as if you were carrying around a jigsaw puzzle piece looking for a place to fit it in. Ask anyone who will listen as you describe the goal and ask for ideas. This leads to three possible outcomes: the person you ask may have nothing helpful for you, the person may have a more or less related thought that is helpful, or hearing yourself describing your goal to someone else may trigger a useful idea. In fact, anything that gives you a fresh perspective on the goal may lead to fresh options.

Experts in creativity have devised endless numbers of tools that can help you and your collaborators look at a challenge with fresh eyes. For example, the book *What a Great Idea 2.0* by Chic Thompson offers more than 250 pages of quick, easy ways to unlock your creativity. Browse the book, pick a technique, and try it out.

TEST YOUR UNDERSTANDING

Instructions:

Read the collaboration between a coach and a sales professional below. Then mark certain sections as follows:

G for any section where the coach seeks to verify *Goals*

S for any section where there is an attempt to *Suspend restrictions*

C for any section where *Connections and patterns* were acknowledged

P for any section demonstrating patience with the creative process

Coach:	So let's set a goal of devising a "note to self" that will be loud and clear to you, but meaningless and inconspicuous to anyone else—no matter what languages they know.
Sales professional:	I could write really tiny.
Coach:	I'll make a list. Keep going ... *Tiny writing.* No restrictions—let's capture as many ideas as we can in five minutes, and then we'll see what we have.
Sales professional:	Okay, but if I write tiny I probably won't notice it in time. Doesn't meet the loud-and-clear test.
Coach:	Don't edit now. Let's just dump ideas. Quantity over quality. I'm going to add to the list to find an emoji of an ear to remind you to listen.

Sales professional:	Dumping ideas reminded me of feature dumping. How about an emoji of a dump truck with a slash through it—no dumping?
Coach:	Good. More.
Sales professional:	I get it! Basically, I gave up too soon on my original idea of a "note to self." I will try one of these approaches on my next call and keep refining as necessary.

Answer Key

Instructions:

Read the collaboration between a coach and a sales professional below. Then mark certain sections as follows:

G for any section where the coach seeks to verify *Goals*

S for any section where there is an attempt to *Suspend restrictions*

C for any section where *Connections and patterns* were acknowledged

P for any section demonstrating patience with the creative process

---

Coach:	So let's set a goal of devising a "note to self" that will be loud and clear to you, but meaningless and inconspicuous to anyone else – no matter what languages they know.

Sales professional:	I could write really tiny.

Coach:	I'll make a list. Keep going ... *Tiny writing.*
S	No restrictions – let's capture as many ideas as we can in five minutes and then we'll see what we have.

Sales professional:	Okay, but if I write tiny I probably won't notice it in time. Doesn't meet the "loud and clear" test.

Coach:	Don't edit now. Let's just dump ideas. Quantity over quality.
	I'm going add to the list to find an emoji of an ear for "listen."

Sales professional: *C*	Dumping ideas reminded me of "feature dumping." How about an emoji of a dump truck with a slash through it "no dumping?"
Coach: *P*	Good. More.
Sales professional:	I get it! Basically I gave up too soon on my original idea of a "note-to-self." I will try one of these approaches on my next call, and keep refining as necessary.

What makes innovation difficult?

Standard approaches include standard assumptions and restrictions and standard ways of analyzing. Those are the disciplined modes of thinking that enable you to measure, fine-tune, polish, troubleshoot, and fix. Innovation involves at least considering breaking the rules. To tap into the parts of your mind that are not limited by standard ways of thinking, you and your conversation partners can temporarily suspend those standard approaches. For most people, most of the time, the habits of rational thinking enable us to do our jobs. And disorganized thinking, rule-breaking, or even *considering* rule-breaking, may produce paralyzing anxiety. If the time spent with restrictions suspended does produce anxiety, set a time limit for that phase and take comfort in the knowledge that you will return to a more structured process when that time is up.

We may also fear that expressing strange or foolish-sounding ideas will open us to disapproval by others. **Should we waste our colleagues' time with ideas that defy common sense?** Our ability to apply standard solutions and familiar thought patterns saves enormous amounts of time and energy. We don't have to start from scratch to figure out how to meet every challenge. But that same ability may get in the way of seeing new patterns and solutions. You need both ways of thinking.

Deliberate Professionalism

It is one thing to read about, talk about, and even practice a set of communications skills. It is quite another thing to deploy those skills in the heat of the moment. Coaching conversations are high-stakes activities. Your intent is always to help your salespeople get better at what they do. But you can also have the opposite effect. As you get ready to launch your next coaching conversation, do a final check of your mind-set:

- *Active Listening* is just as essential as anything you might say.
- Don't fall behind in *Expressing Praise*.
- *Express* your *Concerns* with both candor and precision.
- *Inviting Innovation* will enhance your sales professional's options and the collaborative relationship that you share.

Questions for
Reflection

QUESTIONS FOR REFLECTION ABOUT
THE CASE FOR PROFESSIONAL COMMUNICATION SKILLS

1. If you completely lost the ability to communicate, what percent of your job could you still do?

   _____

   _____

   _____

2. Do the people you coach ever misinterpret what you say?

   _____

   _____

   _____

3. A conversation between a sales coach and the person receiving the coaching requires effort by both parties to avoid misunderstanding and unintended effects. Should that effort be born equally between the two parties, or should one of the parties bear a greater share? If so, who should bear the greater effort, and how much greater?

   _____

   _____

   _____

4. What are some potentially poor outcomes from a coaching conversation?

   _____

   _____

   _____

Questions for Reflection about *Active Listening*

1. Describe a consequence you have experienced as a result of poor listening.

   _____

   _____

   _____

   _____

   _____

2. *Active Listening* consists of three steps. If you could magically become perfect at only one of those steps, which one would you choose and why?

   _____

   _____

   _____

   _____

   _____

3. Can you think of other reasons why *Active Listening* is sometimes difficult?

   _____

   _____

   _____

   _____

   _____

   _____

QUESTIONS FOR REFLECTION ABOUT
EXPRESSING PRAISE

1. List one or two of the top reasons why you might be reluctant to express praise, even when you know it might enhance the effectiveness of your coaching.

   _____

   _____

   _____

2. Think from your experience of a time when you received praise for your work:

   Did that praise include all four elements?

   _____

   _____

   _____

   How did that praise affect you?

   _____

   _____

   _____

3. Think from your experience of a time when you felt that your performance deserved praise, but <u>you did not receive any</u>. Now craft an expression of praise that you would like to have received at that time. Include all four steps.

   _____

   _____

   _____

QUESTIONS FOR REFLECTION ABOUT *EXPRESSING CONCERN*

1. Why would you confirm relevant goals before expressing concern?

_____

_____

_____

_____

_____

_____

2. If the person to whom you are expressing concern does not share your goals, is there any point to expressing your concern?

_____

_____

_____

_____

_____

3. In what ways do *Active Listening* and *Expressing Concern* overlap?

_____

_____

_____

_____

_____

Questions for Reflection about
Inviting Innovation

1. What benefits do you see of crafting and writing down a goal statement for a creative collaboration?

_____

_____

_____

_____

2. Why does Step 2 say, "*Suspend…*" rather than, "*Eliminate…*"?

_____

_____

_____

_____

3. Share any examples that you can remember of another person's idea triggering you to have an idea.

_____

_____

_____

_____

4. What can you do to recognize or protect an idea when another person in your conversation dismisses it?

_____

_____

_____

_____

Level 5 Communication Skills

Active Listening

When:

You will take action or make a decision.
You feel triggered to **reject, ignore or disagree.**

1. Presume value.
2. Explore what and why.
3. Verify your understanding of what and why.

Expressing Praise

When:

You appreciate the quality, reliability or improvement in someone's work.

1. Refer to specific *praise-worthy* performance.
2. Cite examples.
3. Connect to personal qualities.
4. Connect to goals.

Expressing Concern

When:

An idea, request or performance seems flawed or concerning to you.

1. Confirm shared and/or conflicting goals.
2. Itemize both elements of value and your concerns.
3. Invite/offer ways to eliminate concerns while retaining value.

Inviting Innovation

When:

A performer seems stuck and needs a breakthrough to overcome a performance challenge.
You want additional or better options.

1. Verify goal(s).
2. Suspend restrictions and judgments.
3. Recognize and connect ideas/patterns.
4. Express patience.

Level 5 Communication Skills

Key Concepts

Start with the presumption of value. If you don't see how a coworker's idea or action serves your shared goals, ask.

Your strong impulse to reject, ignore or disagree is a valuable cue to presume value.

Useful Phrases

1. What is the goal of your suggestion?

2. If I understand your idea correctly, you suggest that...

3. What you have accomplished here contributes to our goal of...

4. What's most important to me is ... Tell me what's most important to you.

5. I see how your idea would help with ... My concern is that ...

6. Let's take 10 minutes right now and see if we can creatively come up with ways to serve both goals.

7. What if there were no limits on time, budget and/or space?

8. What's the best you could do if it absolutely had to be ready by noon tomorrow?

9. Your idea of ... makes me think that maybe we could ...

10. Let's sleep on it.

Other books available on Amazon by Level Five Selling

Level Five Selling is for sales leaders who want to dramatically increase their odds of exceeding their quota year after year. However, it is equally relevant for sales trainers, who want to increase the certainty of a payback on the training programs they build or buy. Finally, it also applies to sales representatives who seek to master the art of selling, earn top commissions, and enjoy the recognition associated with being number one on the sales leader board.

The Level Five Coaching System provides a road map for sales enablement managers and sales leaders to follow when implementing a documented and fully implemented process for coaching and developing preeminent sales teams. This system provides the frontline sales leaders with the method, skills, tools, and resources to execute dynamic coaching. In addition, this book offers a step-by-step formula and specific "how to's" for any sized sales organization to improve win rates, reduce turnover, reduce ramp to productivity time, and meet and exceed your top-line revenue targets.

If a company expects its sales leaders to meet or exceed its revenue goals, they must be outstanding recruiters, trainers, and coaches. So, we wrote **The Level Five Sales Leader** to share our insights gained from our combined decades of sales consulting experience, helping sales leaders to achieve that goal. If you focus on these critical success factors of frontline sales leaders. In that case, we firmly believe you will see dramatic improvements in sales results, less turnover, higher win rates, and more satisfied and loyal customers.

Sales leaders who consistently perform at the top of their game are collaborative coaches and outstanding communicators.

If you fail to:

- Understand your sales professional's point of view; you stand little chance of winning them to your point of view.
- Explicitly call attention to your sales professional's strengths, progress, and successes; you squander opportunities to encourage more positive behavior.
- Clearly and directly express disagreement or calling out counter-productive behavior or performance, you deny your sales professionals the information they need to make progress.

On the other hand, if you establish and maintain collaborative coaching relationships with your salespeople and invite innovation, they flourish.

Contact Us

You can bulk purchase the books at a discount by contacting us. To learn more about how Level Five Selling helps frontline sales leaders become masterful sales coaches, please contact us at info@levelfiveselling.com or 800-975-6768 David Pearson Ext 701 John Hoskins Ext 702. www.levelfiveselling.com.

We would welcome a call to discuss your needs.

Made in the USA
Middletown, DE
18 November 2022